Newswriting Guide

DATE DUE

SEP 1 3 2008	

Newswriting Guide

✦

A Handbook for Student Reporters

Fourth Edition

Rachel Bard

iUniverse, Inc.

New York Lincoln Shanghai

Newswriting Guide
A Handbook for Student Reporters

Copyright © 2005 by Rachel Bard

iUniverse books may be ordered through booksellers or by contacting:

iUniverse
2021 Pine Lake Road, Suite 100
Lincoln, NE 68512
www.iuniverse.com
1-800-Authors (1-800-288-4677)
Or
Literary Network Press
P.O. Box 13523
Burton, WA 98013

first printing January 1980
second printing December 1982
second edition, third printing January 1988
third edition, fourth printing July 1992
fourth edition November 2005

ISBN-13: 978-0-595-37484-7 (pbk)
ISBN-13: 978-0-595-81877-8 (ebk)
ISBN-10: 0-595-37484-0 (pbk)
ISBN-10: 0-595-81877-3 (ebk)

Printed in the United States of America

This book grew out of the needs of the staff of the Collegiate Challenge, published by the students of Tacoma Community College. To my students who were eager to learn and receptive to the idea of a written handbook, thank you.

Thanks also to my successors in the TCC Journalism Department, who proved through use of the book that it served a purpose; and to other journalism instructors and publication advisers all over the country, who have continued to use the book and make valuable suggestions.

In particular, as I prepared this edition I received valuable counsel from Greg McElroy, journalism instructor at Vashon Senior High School and David Holman, Faculty Adviser for the Challenge at TCC.

I also thank my colleagues at Literary Network Press for their generous assistance in publishing the book.

Rachel Bard
Vashon Island, Washington

Contents

Introduction

This is a handbook for student writers and would-be writers who have had little or no training in newswriting (or need refreshing), and who must become productive reporters for a school newspaper, fast.

It's also designed for anybody with no prior experience in publicity writing who is called on to publicize a club, organization, company or individual; it will help such persons to write acceptable news stories.

It will be useful to the desktop publisher of newsletters and bulletins who may have more skill in the creative aspects of layout, design, printing and production than in the writing itself.

It would be desirable, of course, if all beginners had some previous instruction in journalism. But often this isn't possible and they are forced to plunge in and learn the hard way. With a short, concise guide to the elementary, widely accepted rules and customs of the newspaper world, the path may be slightly smoothed. Hence this handbook, covering the 10 aspects of newswriting that seem to give the most trouble to beginning reporters.

Now a few words about what this book is not. Since most staff members of school newspapers are busy, overworked people with little time to study textbooks, this is not a textbook. Many excellent journalism texts exist. Some explore the theory of communications. Most explain why newspapers are written the way they are. And nearly all include practical exercises and projects for developing and improving newswriting skill. This book does none of these things. As soon as possible, every neophyte reporter should consult a good journalism textbook. See the list on page 45 for a start. Also listed are a few helpful reference works found on the desks of most experienced journalists.

Thus, this is neither a comprehensive textbook nor an infallible guide. Though the writing hints and story formats presented here conform with widely followed journalistic practice, there are no absolute rules in journalism, as there are in Latin or algebra, for example. Nearly everyone in the field, whether editor, reporter, or teacher, has a different idea of the right way to write. The rules and guidelines you'll find here do agree with those observed in most newsrooms and classrooms. But don't be surprised or alarmed if your editor or adviser or instructor has a different view.

Therefore, this guide won't help you strike out on new and dazzling creative paths. It will, in fact, confine you, being based on the old-fashioned premise that one should master the conventional wisdom before breaking the rules.

Finally, it's neither objective nor explanatory. It's been deliberately kept short and arbitrary, so you can easily find what you're looking for. That way you'll have more time to write.

1

Newswriting style and format

Even if you master nothing beyond the rules in this chapter, you'll have a good start toward competency in reporting.

/ STYLE

What are "style" rules?

They are simply standards we refer to in deciding how to spell, punctuate, abbreviate, capitalize, etc. They have two purposes:

1. To make newswriting clear and easy to read.

2. To make sure all the writing in a paper follows the same style.

Lack of uniformity in these matters will tend to make the reader suspicious that there may be carelessness and inaccuracy in other areas—and may lead to mistrust in the newspaper in general.

Familiarity with the rules saves time, too. The writer who knows where or whether to use a comma or an abbreviation, or where to look it up in a hurry, need not stop to wonder about it or ask others, but can devote his or her time to the real business at hand—being a reporter. And correct style on the part of the reporter saves the editor's time in making corrections.

Every paper has its own style, and many have their own stylebooks. Most use the AP Stylebook, with modifications to suit their own editor's quirks or customs. Another widely used book is that of The New York Times.

Though you need not memorize any stylebook, you should become familiar enough with it to be able to find the answers quickly. The sections you will need to refer to most are: numerals, capitalization, punctuation, abbreviations and spelling. You should also be thoroughly familiar with your own paper's style rules.

The next chapter is a miniature stylebook, for your quick reference.

But good newswriting style goes far beyond adherence to rules about commas, capital letters, etc. In the broader sense a newspaper reporter's style should be such that the reader is given the facts quickly, logically, clearly and objectively. At the same time the reporter tries to make the story interesting. That's no small order. But your style will improve as you keep writing, and reading good newswriting in other papers.

A few suggestions:

1. Omit needless words. (Strunk and White, whose book is listed in Chapter 12, have good counsel on this in Chapter II, No. 17.) Almost any first draft can be cut and tightened and will be a better piece of work as a result.

2. Use the active voice rather than the passive.

3. Use the right word, the precise word. Don't guess. If you aren't sure, substitute another word, or look your word up.

4. Don't express your own opinion or render judgements. Avoid use of "I" or "me" (except in quotes). (See Chapter 11.)

// FORMAT

Each publication sets its own standards for copy format. Yours may differ considerably from these, which are typical but not universal.

1. Double space.

2. Indent all paragraphs five spaces.

3. Don't use spaces between paragraphs.

4. In upper left corner, type:

    a. File name.

    b. Your name

    c. Date you turn in the story.

    d. Slugline—subject of story, as Jazz concert, or Mayor's speech.

5. Place your name and page number at top of each succeeding page.

6. Use wide margins, at least an inch, on all sides.

7. Avoid keyboard formatting.

8. To show that the story is continued on another page, type (more) at the bottom of the page.

9. Under the end of the story type an end mark:-30-or #.

10. Use the spellchecker, but don't depend on it to be infallible.

11. Read your finished story, preferably a print-out, and correct errors.

2

Style rules

Here are the 13 areas most likely to cause confusion as you write your stories, and a few basic rules in each area to help you conform to widely accepted practices on the best newspapers in the country.

However, you should always have the AP Stylebook (or whatever stylebook your paper uses as final authority) for further reference and amplification. And, of course, use the dictionary freely.

/ NUMBERS

1. In general, use numerals for 10 and over. Spell out under 10. This applies to both cardinal and ordinal numbers.

   (See exceptions below.)

   Examples:

   Each team must win three games within the next 30 days.

   It was the third inning.

   The 212th domino fell.

2. However, spell out all numbers used in certain common and casual expressions.

   Examples:

   a million-to-one chance

   no, no, ten thousand times no!

   a thousand and one uses (Never a 1,000 and one uses.)

   sweet sixteen

3. Use numerals for ages, temperatures, dimensions, heights, times, sports scores, speeds and all numbers that contain decimals, even if under 10.

    Examples:

    A 9-year-old boy was injured. His brother, 14, was not hurt.

    High and low temperatures yesterday were 90° in Phoenix, AZ and 5° in Estes Park, CO.

    A 5-by-10-foot box fell out.

    The 6-foot-10-inch guard was the star of the evening. (Note use of hyphens when dimensions are used adjectivally before a noun.)

    The procession started at 6 p.m. Monday, moving at about 3 miles per hour.

    The Mariners won by a score of 5 to 3.

    The average family size is 3.5 persons.

4. If a numeral begins a sentence it must be spelled out. It is often preferable to rewrite the sentence, for the sake of brevity—a good quality in newswriting.

    Examples:

    Seven hundred and seventy-six years ago, the Moors lost this decisive battle to the Christians.

    The Moors lost this decisive battle to the Christians 776 years ago.

5. However, if a calendar year starts the sentence it need not be spelled out.

    Example:

    1212 was a bad year for the Moors in Spain.

// PERCENTAGES

1. Percent is now written as one word if you go by the AP Stylebook. Always spell it out; never use the % symbol (except in headlines).

2. Always use figures in percentages, even if the number is less than 10. If the figure is not a whole number use decimals, not fractions.

Examples:

His popularity dropped by 2 percent.

Tuition will increase 5.5 percent next year.

Tuition rise of 5.5% predicted (headline)

/// MONEY

1. The $ sign is permitted but the ¢ sign is not. Never spell out the word dollar or dollars, unless used without figures, or with rounded-off or indefinite large amounts.

Examples:

The fee is $2 per person.

It's simply a matter of dollars and cents.

a cool quarter of a million dollars

2. In large amounts over $1 million, use a decimal after the million, then round off with one or two figures, deleting all the zeros.

Example:

The deficit is forecast at $2.25 million, rather than the originally estimated $2.3 million.

3. For amounts under $1, use figures and spell out the word cents. Never (we repeat) use the ¢ symbol.

Example:

The booklets cost 50 cents, with an additional 5 cents for wrapping.

IV TIME

1. Use lower case and periods in a.m. and p.m. and always use figures, except for noon and midnight. Avoid unnecessary zeros or words.

   Example:

   The session started at 10 a.m. (*not* ten a.m. or 10:00 a.m.), recessed at noon (*not* 12:00 noon) and resumed at 1:15 p.m.

2. Avoid o'clock. If you do use it, it's better not to use a.m. or p.m. with it, but to refer to morning, afternoon or evening.

   Example:

   It was still burning at 4 o'clock this morning.

V TITLES

First, the everyday or "courtesy" titles: Mr., Mrs., Ms. Different newspapers have different rules for how to treat them.

1. If you go by Associated Press style, you will never use Mr. in a news story, except with Mrs.

   Example:

   Mr. and Mrs. James Wheeler received the award, after which Wheeler gave an acceptance speech.

2. Many papers now omit the "courtesy title" for women too. If yours does, on first reference use the woman's given name and last name, thereafter just her last name, with no title.

   Example:

   Janice Hedlund's latest book, "Looking at Ourselves," received mixed reviews. It's all the same to Hedlund—she's hard at work on her next book.

3. But some papers recommend asking the woman what her preference is: Mrs., Miss, Ms. or no title at all. This is one more thing to remember during the interview, but it is usually appreciated.

VI "REAL" TITLES

Abbreviation and capitalization are the critical areas.

1. Abbreviate and capitalize most formal titles when they precede the name, but not when used without the name. (See AP Stylebook for military titles that are not abbreviated.)

    Examples:

    Before Gov. Howard appeared the lieutenant governor spoke briefly, then introduced the governor.

    The captain saluted the admiral.

    Gen. Eisenhower's term as president preceded the troubled '60s.

    Dr. Jonas Salk is remembered for his role in the battle against polio.

    Rep. Jane Perdue, a three-term representative from the fifth district, was re-elected.

    The measure will not pass, Sen. Mitchell predicted.

2. Do not abbreviate president when used preceding a name and always capitalize when referring to the incumbent president of the United States.

    Example:

    He said President Lincoln was more widely quoted than any other president.

VII MONTHS, DATES, DAYS OF WEEK

1. Abbreviate the month only if it is followed by the date; but always spell out March, April, May, June and July.

    Example:

    Work-study students should submit time sheets between Feb. 25 and March 1 in order to be paid for February work.

2. In dates, always use numerals without suffixes (th, nd, st, rd).

    Example:

    This nation was born on July 4,1776. (But: the Fourth of July)

3. Never abbreviate days of the week.

    Example:

    The play will open Wednesday, Oct. 22.

VIII APOSTROPHE

This is one of the most abused punctuation marks, because it has two quite different functions and they are easy to confuse. The apostrophe indicates a deleted letter, as in a contraction, and also indicates the possessive.

First, to show deletions:

1. Use the apostrophe in contractions to show deletion of a letter or letters.

    Examples:

    It's too early to say when the playground will be opened.

    "I don't agree!" he shot back.

2. Use the apostrophe to show deletion of figures.

    Examples:

    a movie about the '50s

    the class of '89

Second, the apostrophe for possessives:

1. Use it with s for possessives of nouns and proper names.

    Examples:

    Snarkey's son took on the city's best fighters.

    Women's volleyball starts next week.

2. If a common noun ends with s in the singular, you still add 's to make it possessive.

    Examples:

    the bus's exhaust

    the shepherdess's flock

3. If a proper name ends in s in the singular, add only the apostrophe to make it possessive.

    Examples:

    Tom Ross' house

    Dr. Stevens' remarks

    James' dog

4. Never use the apostrophe in possessive pronouns.

    Examples:

    The dog chased its tail.

    She said the ring was hers.

    Whose was the fault, if not yours?

IX QUOTES

1. The comma and the period always go inside end quotes.

    Examples:

    "The staff should serve the students," she said.

    The drama department will present "Julius Caesar."

    "Were it not for the money," Rorum said, "I would quit this job."

2. Other punctuation marks go inside quotes when they apply to the quoted matter only. They go outside if they apply to the whole sentence.

    Examples:

Did he ask, "Is it time?" or did he say, "It is time"?

Will it be "business as usual"? The chairman would not say.

The chairman was asked, "Will it be business as usual?"

According to the sheriff, the man will be charged with "criminal negligence; driving without a license, while under the influence; neglect of official duty"; and several minor charges.

"What a day for a parade!" the mayor said.

"I would like to thank"—at this point Martin began to break down—"the Yankee management, the players"—here he began crying.

3. Use quotation marks around titles of books, plays, movies, poems, songs, musical works, TV program titles and speech titles, but not newspapers or magazines.

    Example:

    The Los Angeles Times printed the schedule of performances, including "The Fantasticks" and Leonard Bernstein's "Mass."

4. Quoted material inside a quote is set off by single quotation marks.

    Example:

    Jameson said, "As I understand the term 'private enterprise,' it permits no governmental intervention of this nature."

5. Use single quotes in headlines.

    Example:

    Farber calls verdict 'unacceptable'

X Capitalization

When in doubt, don't capitalize. The trend in journalism now is toward the "down style"—lower case.

1. Do not capitalize names of college courses or classes, except languages.

    Example:

The curriculum includes algebra, biology, English, nursing and French.

2.   Do not capitalize seasons.

Example:

He will resign after spring quarter and will be replaced by fall.

3.   Do not capitalize titles when used without the name, and do not capitalize titles that are really descriptive or occupational designations.

Examples:

Both Sen. Bradley and Rep. Swift expect the vote to be taken tomorrow. However, the senator was pessimistic about passage.

Harry Sawyer, chief engineer on the project, could not be reached.

Efforts to reach engineer Harry Sawyer, in charge of the project, were futile.

television personality Barbara Walters

attorney Bill Barker (But: District Attorney Janet Hawthorne)

XI ADDRESSES

1.   Abbreviate Street, Avenue and Boulevard only when used with the street number, and always use figures for the street number.

Examples:

He works at 666 Maidenvale Blvd.

Sunset Boulevard has much in common with 42nd Street.

The crime occurred at 73 Ames St., near Cedar Avenue.

2.   Spell out numbered street names, through nine; for higher numbers use figures.

Examples:

721 First Ave.

900 12th St.

3. Spell out other address designations: Terrace, Place, Circle, Drive, Road, with or without street numbers.

Examples:

51 Sunset Terrace, the corner of Carlton Place and Columbus Circle, 41 East Drive, on Mountain View Road

4. Abbreviate East, West, South and North when used as part of the street name, when the street number is used. Otherwise spell out.

Examples:

The fire was at 711 S. Main St.

It was on South Main Street.

5. When incorporating an Internet address in a story (e-mail address or Web site), and the address falls at the end of a sentence, use a period. If the address must be continued from one line to the next, break it before a slash or a dot, and never use a hyphen.

Examples:

More information is available at http://oregonstate.edu.

For more information, contact jopage@homeservice or call 228-2288.

XII SPELLING

There is no excuse for a misspelled word in the copy you turn in to your editor. If you have the shadow of a doubt, even after using the spell checker, look in your dictionary. You will also find the correct spelling of many commonly misspelled words in the AP Stylebook, in appropriate alphabetical locations. For quick reference, and commitment to memory, here are a few words that many people have trouble with.

a lot	consensus	liaison
accommodate	consistent	memento
achieve	disappoint	missile
anyone	embarrass	proponents

barbecue	enroll	receive
cannot	enrollment	sponsor
category	harass	weird

XIII SUFFIXES, PREFIXES

1. Most suffixes are written solid, without a hyphen.

    Examples:

    threefold, operagoer, statewide

2. So are most prefixes, but there are many exceptions. When in doubt about whether to hyphenate a prefix, follow the general rule not to hyphenate unless the prefix ends in the same vowel that the following word begins with.

    Examples:

antifreeze	overpower	rephrase
antebellum	nonaligned	anti-inflationary
bimonthly	postwar	pre-existing
coexist	preconceived	re-educate
excommunicate	semiweekly	
interstate	sublet	

3. Exceptions to the above rule:

    a. No hyphen in cooperate or coordinate.

    b. Certain words take co with the hyphen to show occupation or status, as in co-author, co-pilot.

    c. Ex, when meaning former, takes a hyphen, as in ex-president.

3

Editing copy

Always read your copy carefully before turning it in. This is your last chance not only to correct errors, but also to improve your work. You as the writer are responsible for your story: its logical organization, completeness, accuracy, correct style and absence of errors. Look for ways to shorten and improve your writing.

A copy editor will read it too, and there is usually another final check (proofreading) before it is printed in the paper. When your copy editor returns your story you will probably find it marked up with standard copyreading symbols to show you what changes should be made. Sometimes you may be called on to edit other writers' copy. Whether as writer or editor, you should be familiar with these symbols, universally used to save time and space in editing copy (also see table page 51).

To delete letters or words:

> "Tomorrow is an~~n~~other day," said
> ~~remarked~~ the general.

Another way to delete a letter or punctuation mark:

> It's tail was wagging.

To transpose letters or words:

If only we could see easily into hte future!

To capitalize a lower-case letter:

The meeting is set for wednesday.

To make a capital letter lower-case:

There is no Team support.

To abbreviate a word or the name of an organization, or to spell out a figure or an abbreviation (the same symbol is used in both cases, and simply means do the opposite):

The 3 members of the United States Department of State were the secy. asst. secy. and a translator.

To join letters or words:

Crime is on t he in crease.

To separate two letters with a space:

Crime is onthe increase.

To indicate new paragraph:

> The financial subcommittee met Thursday
> to consider next year's budget.|Before the
> meeting, members were handed two
> versions of the proposal.

To join the end of one paragraph to the beginning of the next:

> The subcommittee met Thursday to
> consider next year's budget.
>
> Before the meeting, members were given
> two versions of the proposal.

To insert a period:

> Think about it (or: Think about it.)

To insert other punctuation:

> Think about it she urged.

To insert a letter:

> liason

To insert a word:

> Say what you really mean.

To correct a misspelling, cross out wrong letter and place correct letter above, with an inverted caret:

> The exhibits are in two catagorys.

To make a deletion and then link the two portions of the sentence, when they are on different lines:

> The exhibits are in two categories (which were selected by the gallery manager), but one more may be added.

To insert a hyphen:

> She is an eight year old girl.

To indicate a dash:

> If you are right and I believe you are you must act at once.

4

How to write a news story: the lead

The lead—that is, the first dozen or so words—carries 90 percent of the burden of the whole story. Since your first purpose is to get the reader interested and involved, you must tell at once what is most important, most newsworthy, most unusual. The lesser facts can follow.

Leads are not easy to write. You must think about all the facts you have gathered, then ask yourself:

What is the main news? What is the most important and most recent? What has *just* happened to make this worth writing about? How can I summarize it in as few words as possible?

The standard news lead, then, is a quick summary of what the story is all about. It is usually only one sentence and never more than one paragraph.

/ *FIRST THINGS FIRST*

The summary lead or standard news lead is still the most common type. Originally this kind of lead answered five or six questions: who, what, where, when, how, and sometimes why. In today's newswriting you need not squeeze all those facts into your lead. But you should decide which are most important, and build your lead around them, so that the most important fact is first.

For example, look at these two leads for the same story:

Lead 1:
Yesterday the presidential selection committee met at the McCormick Conference Center, screened the 50 applicants for the position of college president to five finalists and announced that the final selection would be made within two weeks.

(An attempt to crowd all the facts in, without placing most important ones first.)

Lead 2 (better):
The new president of Basin College will be named within two weeks, the presidential selection committee announced yesterday.
(**Who** is most important; put it first)

In deciding which fact to put first, remember that names make news, and readers want to know "what happened?"

Usually, therefore, the *who* or the *what* will come first. Once in a while the *when* or *where* will be most important, and less frequently, the *how* or *why*.

After sorting out your facts and writing your lead sentence to emphasize the most important ones, follow at once with the others. For example, the sentence after Lead 2 above could read:

The committee, meeting at the McCormick Conference Center, screened 50 applications and agreed on five finalists, from whom the successful candidate will be chosen.

Sometimes, of course, you can answer all the questions in your lead if the story is an uncomplicated one:

James Connelly said yesterday at a press conference at Inland Bank that he is stepping down as president because he feels it is "time for new blood."

// BE SHORT

Some say a lead should be no longer than 29 words; others say no more than four typed lines. These are pretty good rules of thumb. If you have written more than four lines, see if you can't cut some words. Some pointers on cutting:

Any lead that starts with "There is," "There was," "There were," etc. can usually be shortened.

For example:

Lead 1:
There will be a special meeting of the Black Students Union at 3 p.m. Thursday to hear proposals for the organization's new constitution.

Lead 2 (better):
The Black Students Union will meet Thursday to consider a new constitution.

Changing from the passive to active voice is another way to strengthen and shorten your lead.

Lead 1:
A concert of 20th-century guitar music will be presented by John Williams tomorrow at the Playhouse.

Lead 2 (better):
John Williams will play 20th-century guitar music at the Playhouse tomorrow.

/// OTHER KINDS OF LEADS

Though the summary news lead is probably the easiest way to begin a news story, there are other ways, including:

Quotation: If you start with a quote, be sure it is short and informative and that it summarizes the news adequately. It should meet the same tests as the summary news lead: involve the reader and let him or her know what the news is.

For example:

"Twenty years are enough," said James Connelly, president of Inland Bank, announcing his retirement yesterday.

Question: Make it brief and provocative. Don't use a question because you are too lazy to write a good standard news lead.

For example:

Can the destruction of the world's rain forests be slowed before they are all gone? Most conferees at the International Resources Council meeting in Brussels have expressed serious doubts.

Most other types of leads are generally more appropriate for features, interviews, humorous or suspended-interest stories. For example, you will often observe use of the descriptive lead (describing a person or a place) or the anecdote lead (starting with a short story that sets the stage or illustrates some aspect of your news) in the non-straight news story.

5

How to write a news story: the body

After the lead, you get down to business with the body of the story.

Most news stories are written in inverted pyramid form. The lead is at the top, the "heaviest" part. Then the other facts follow in descending order of importance, all the way to the least important fact, which makes the bottom point of the pyramid.

This is called writing in logical order, starting with the most essential facts, then giving supporting details to explain the lead, then continuing with additional facts or incidents, down to the most expendable, which come last.

When you finish presenting all your facts, in logical order, stop. News stories do not end with summaries or conclusions.

Very occasionally you will want to use narrative style, and write the body of the story in chronological order. Your lead should still summarize the most important, recent events; then tell the whole story in chronological order, start to finish. This format is effective when you have a strong "story line" and are reporting dramatic events such as accidents, fires or sports.

Each paragraph in the story should incorporate a complete thought and should not depend on the next paragraph to explain it. And it should be possible for the reader to stop after any paragraph and still have read an intelligible, complete story. To continue the inverted pyramid analogy, each step of the pyramid is an "exit"—a term used by journalists to describe the point where the reader can leave the story and still have a clear understanding of its import.

/ *TRANSITIONS*

Though each paragraph in the story is a complete thought, it should lead logically to the next one. The story should become a unified whole, not be a series of disconnected facts or incidents or quotations. So transitional words and phrases and sentences are often necessary, to avoid confusing the reader with a new and unrelated thought.

Sometimes just a word will bridge the gap, such as: but, meanwhile, however, nevertheless, later, again, also. Sometimes you need a whole paragraph.

Example of transitional word:

> **A new downtown bus depot will be built this summer at 12th and Atlantic to serve suburban line riders. The Transit Commission voted at its monthly meeting yesterday to erect the building, which will be completed by September.**
>
> **The Commission also agreed to purchase four new trolley buses to add to the city fleet.**

(*Also* links the second paragraph to the first.)

Transitional paragraph:

> **The legislature passed a bill yesterday to prohibit smoking in all public places.**
>
> **Janice Farrell, president of Citizens Concerned about Smoking, hailed the bill as a "great step forward in our fight against cancer." Most administrators contacted have said they welcome the prohibition and expect it to be effective.**
>
> **But at least one had a different reaction.**
>
> **Gil Roth, manager of the Capitol Restaurant said, "Maybe they voted for it, but a lot of the legislators will have second thoughts when they come in here for a cup of coffee or a beer and can't light up."**

(The third paragraph prepares for the shift to a quote in the fourth paragraph.)

// USE OF QUOTES

Quotations enliven a story and make it more real and believable to the reader. But don't use quotations unless (1) they add something newsworthy, and say it succinctly and colorfully, or (2) the subject is controversial or technical, and you want to use the speaker's exact words, to avoid misunderstanding.

Examples:

Coach Lemke reminisced, "The relay team came over the hurdles like hound dogs after a coon."

"There's no excuse for such flagrant dereliction of duty on the part of the police chief," Mayor Jorgenson said.

Every quote must be attributed to the source; that is, say who said it. Never take a chance that the reader can figure out where the statement or information came from. This goes for indirect quotes as well as direct.

Example:

A Union Pacific train derailed near Centralia today, with three cars leaving the track but no injuries. It will be 48 hours before service can resume, according to James Morris, Northwest manager for the railroad.

Avoid excessive use of quotes, for the sake of brevity. Usually you can paraphrase (put in your own words) or summarize a speaker's remarks in far fewer words than were actually used.

If you have a lot of quoted material that you want to include, two good rules are to alternate direct and indirect quotes; and not to use more than two consecutive paragraphs of direct quotation.

6

Interviewing

Almost every news story requires you to get information by asking questions. Maybe your entire story depends on this kind of information, or maybe you need only a few more facts. But in either case you need to know how to ask questions, that is, how to interview.

Here are some pointers to help you plan your attack.

1. Use the phone to find out who your best source or sources will be, rather than trotting around unannounced to look up people you think might be helpful. Often, you may be able to conduct the entire interview by phone.

2. Whether making an appointment or beginning a phone interview, explain at once who you are and why you want the interview.

3. Read up on your subject. Use the Internet to get background information. Look up back copies of the newspaper if the subject is local, and learn enough so you won't have to annoy the person you're interviewing by asking questions about the obvious. For example, you should never have to ask someone's first name, job or title.

4. Write out your questions in advance. Even if you don't refer to them during the interview this helps you organize and plan. Don't hesitate to deviate from your list of questions if your source says something that opens up a new subject or train of thought that is pertinent to your story.

5. Take notes, as many as you can without losing track of what is being said. Develop your own system of abbreviations and rapid writing. You'll improve with practice. If you're using the phone near your computer, you can learn to take notes directly on the keyboard.

6. Take down as many direct quotes as you can—more than you need. You will want them to give life to your story. So whenever your subject says something particularly apt, colorful, succinct, controversial or otherwise noteworthy, take it down as accurately as you can. If you're in doubt, don't hesitate to ask him or her to repeat it or let you read it back. Most people are flattered that you want to use their exact words. Some won't be, and will tell you they don't wish to be quoted. You will have to respect their wishes.

7. Take notes on your subject's appearance, mannerisms, surroundings and dress, for use in descriptive phrases or sentences in your story.

8. Your questions should be specific, not general. Ask "why?" to draw out more facts and news.

9. Save the tough questions for last.

10. Read your notes over as soon as possible after the interview, and amplify them and make them legible while your memory is fresh. Never let them sit overnight without this review, even if you won't be writing your story until the next day. And at this point (while reviewing your notes), start deciding what was the most newsworthy thing you learned; that will be the lead of your story. Sort out the less important material. Don't feel you must include everything in your notes in your story.

11. Tape recorders? Fine, if taping doesn't make your subject nervous. But there's a disadvantage: it takes a long time to play the tape back, listen, transcribe or take notes; and many news deadlines don't give you that much time.

12. Check back with your source only if you're in doubt about the accuracy of your notes or quotes. Otherwise you should not ask or allow the interviewee to read your draft.

7

Speech stories

A story reporting on a speech is essentially like any other news story, in that it must tell *what happened.* Concentrate on your lead, which must get across what made this speech different from thousands of others. Therefore, tell at once *what* the speaker said, not just *that* he or she made a speech on such-and-such a subject. Never write a lead that tells something your reader already knew or could easily find out.

For example, this is a bad lead for a speech story:

The principal speaker at the National Baristas Association convention last weekend in Atlantic City was Burton Corliss, an economist from the Plato Institute.

Your readers want to know, "What did he say?" A better lead:

In spite of the popularity of espresso cafes, coffee servers' earnings are lagging seriously behind inflation, economist Burton Corliss of the Plato Institute said last weekend. Speaking at the National Baristas Association convention in Atlantic City...

Of course, if you are writing an advance story (before the speech is given), you can't report on what the speaker says, only the subject and what makes the speaker newsworthy:

Burton Corliss, former CEO of Better Beans and now a fellow at the Plato Institute, will address the National Baristas Association convention here next week on "The Crisis in Coffeeshop Compensation."

This is a useful formula for most speech stories: start with a direct or indirect quote that sums up the speaker's views or what was said that was most remarkable. Usually this will be an indirect quote, since few speakers do you the favor of condensing their speeches, neatly and colorfully, in 29 words or less. But you can, if you took good notes, write a concise summary in your own words.

Having disposed of *who* and *what* (the speaker and what he or she said), you must also include *where* and *when* in your lead, and anything else unusual about the circumstances—such as that a standing-room-only audience was present, or that protestors heckled the speaker throughout.

Then the body of your story (if you follow the formula) will alternate your own summaries of parts of the talk with direct quotations.

Use direct quotations when the speaker's words are interesting, startling, controversial, or when they merit verbatim reporting for any other reason. Summarize remarks that are long-winded or in more detail than you need to report. Usually you will write your summary of each of the main topics, then support or illustrate it with a direct quote. Use this format throughout your story, covering all the main topics.

You should also intersperse descriptive and informative passages that add color or interest (such as audience reaction, speaker's manner, notables in the audience, background of the speaker and if necessary, explanations of some references).

Be sure to attribute to the speaker all quotes, especially the indirect ones, to avoid giving the impression that you are presenting information commonly accepted as fact. For example:

The commission chairman said acid rain is not as severe a threat to the world environment as many people claim. Only 9 percent of the forests in North America have been affected, he added.

The last two words are essential. Without them, some readers might accept the statement as proven fact. It may indeed be well documented but you do not have time to look it up, and attribution gets you off the hook.

You need not feel bound to report all the speaker's topics, or to hold to the order in which they were presented. Sometimes speakers save their most newsworthy or important remarks for the end of the speech and you should put them in your lead, reporting the other points in descending order of importance—as in any standard news story.

And, as in any standard news story, you need no summary or conclusion.

8

Reporting on meetings

Here, as in speech stories, you must tell your readers *what happened*. Don't simply report *who* met, but tell what action they took. For example, do not write leads like this:

The Executive Committee of the State Arts Council met yesterday in Sacramento for the monthly financial session.

Instead, tell what the committee did:

A record $600,000 budget for the next biennium was approved by the Executive Committee of the State Arts Council yesterday in Sacramento.

At most meetings several things happen, some more important than others. Don't report them in chronological order, as though you were the secretary writing the minutes. Decide what you think is most important and tell about that in your lead, follow with supporting details, then take up other subjects in descending order of importance.

Even if the meeting seems rather dull, something about it is less dull than the rest. You should be able to find some fresh angle to spark your lead—even if it is simply an unusually large or small attendance.

For example:

A record crowd overflowed the 10,000-seat Chester Stadium last night for the Central States convention of the Horace Walpole Society.

or

Only 13 Clarkston residents turned out to hear the new county comprehensive plan, presented by the Planning Commission at a scheduled public-input hearing last night.

Maybe several things take place at the meeting, all of which you think are equally important. Summarize them all in your lead, then elaborate on each one in the body of your story, in the same order as you listed them in your lead.

For example:

Tuition for resident college students will go up 10 percent next year, but out-of-state students will have it even worse, with a 25 percent raise. The State Board of Higher Education approved the two actions at its monthly public meeting yesterday in Carson City, while postponing action on a faculty salary schedule.

Then you will tell more details on, first, the 10 percent increase for students who are state residents; second, the 25 percent increase for nonresident students; and third, the faculty salary subject.

Just as in a story on a speech, you should observe the proceedings carefully. Ask questions of the participants afterwards, so you can report and explain any events or remarks that will add interest.

For example, later in the same story, rather than simply reporting that the tuition increase passed with a 5–4 vote:

In the 5–4 vote on the resident-student tuition increase, Chairman Johnson surprised his colleagues by switching from his previous position and voting with those in favor.

Also, describe how people look, talk, behave; the surroundings, if at all unusual; and, if there are interruptions, unforeseen incidents (humorous, or of a human-interest or dramatic nature), take note of them, so you will have some meat to add to your story when you sit down to write it.

For example:

While the meeting was going on in Hamilton Hall, a group of students marched outside, chanting and waving "No tuition increase" signs.

Here is a brief checklist of the sorts of newsworthy subjects to look for in covering meetings, which you may consider for your lead or for the body of the story:

Election of officers
Appointment of committees
Passage of laws, ordinances, resolutions
Acceptance of plans, budgets

Discussions, debates (get quotes from both sides, summarize conflicting view-points)

Speeches

Prominent guests and visitors

Musical or other entertainment

Number in attendance

Interruptions

Length of meeting, if unusually short or long

9

Feature stories

A feature differs from a straight news story in two main respects:

One, it need not have a news "peg"—that is, need not report a currently newsworthy event. (Some features do have a news peg, and are called news features.) It is usually interesting for other qualities, such as human interest, humor, the excitement of a true-life adventure, pathos, drama, informativeness, etc.

Two, it has no standard format, and would seldom start with a summary lead or be written in inverted pyramid form. Format is often chronological, and there should be a neat satisfying ending—unlike the straight news story, which has no summary or conclusion or tagline.

But the feature does have two things in common with the news story: it is based on fact, and it must be personally researched by the writer—not rewritten from someone else's published story.

The overall difference is that the news story informs, the feature entertains. Which is not to say that the news story may not be entertaining, or the feature informative.

Though a feature gives you more freedom than a straight news story, it does not permit you to inject your own opinions or editorialize; you are still required to stick to the facts.

Nor does it mean you can indulge in wordiness. Good features are as tightly written as good news stories.

/ *HOW TO BEGIN?*

As in the news story, the lead is the crucial part. You must involve the reader at the start.

If you read enough features in your daily newspaper you'll find that most of them start with one of these:

Quotation

Anecdote
Question
A short intriguing or shocking statement
Description (of person, place or thing)

The temptation to start with a question should be resisted, unless it is truly provocative. And avoid quotations unless they are colorful, startling or otherwise attention-getting.

// SOME TYPES OF FEATURES

Again, study daily papers for features and you will soon see that they fall in various categories, including:

1. Profiles: about a person, often based on an interview. May use description, quotations, biographical facts.

2. Human-interest: also about a person, but not as in-depth as a profile; concentrates on one aspect or event, appealing to reader's emotions: humor, pity, dismay, anger.

3. Travel.

4. Adventure: usually narrative-style.

5. Scientific: explaining how and why in layman's terms, such as why earthquakes occur.

6. Historical: may be timely because of an anniversary of an important date.

7. How-to: telling how to build or do something, such as how to change a washer or grow bean sprouts. May include some first-person experiences.

Here are a few pointers on ways to make your feature story interesting:

1. Have an overall theme.

2. Be specific.

3. Use action verbs.

4. Use devices to liven it up: quotations, little stories, humorous descriptions, startling facts, suspense.

5. Involve the reader by using "you."

6. In your conclusion, return to the theme of your lead.

10

Headlines

In the "real" newspaper world the reporter seldom writes the headline. That's part of the copy editor's job. But anyone may be called on to write heads for the student newspaper, or indeed on many weeklies and small dailies. For the publicity release, a suggested headline helps the editor see at once what the story is about.

Writing the newspaper head is one of the last steps. It comes after the story is written, edited and assigned a spot in the paper, and after a head style has been designated by the editor. This gives the headline writer rigid limits to his creativity:

1. The width of the column and size of type, which determine how many letters per line.

2. The designated style: that is, number of lines; whether head has kicker or deck; whether it is in capitals and lower case, all caps or down style.

First let us define a few of the terms you should understand.

crossline: a one-line head that is centered rather than flush left.

deck: a secondary head under the main head; also called bank.

down style: headline style where only the first letter of the first word, and proper names, are capitalized.

flush left: headline style where all lines of the head begin at the left edge of the column, and may or may not extend to the right edge. However, each line must extend at least half-way across the column.

kicker: a short line above the main head, giving additional facts to amplify the main headline. However, the main head must stand alone and not depend on the kicker to make sense. The kicker is in smaller type than the main head.

head schedule: every paper has its own, showing all combinations of style and size of type. And since column widths differ, the schedule may also show the number of units of each type face and size that will fit in a column. Every paper's schedule is different. Become familiar with yours, and it will save asking a lot of questions.

pulled quote: a quote from the body of the story, used as a three- or **four-line head dropped into a column.**

subhead: a short, one-line headline used to break up the body of the long news story. Use subheads after the first three paragraphs, and no more closely spaced than every three paragraphs

upper and lower case (U and LC) or **caps and lower case:** headline style where the first letter of each important word is capitalized and the rest are in lower case.

/ *WRITING THE HEAD*

You'll find the facts you need in the lead, but read the whole story to make sure you understand what you're summarizing. If your head is to have a deck or kicker, you may find material for this in the body. For example:

Head with a deck:

Hurricane strikes southeastern seaboard
Hundreds of homes destroyed, two dead in South Carolina

Head with a kicker:

Victory comes in final minute
Sonics win crucial
third game,99–97

Your head should be the shortest, punchiest summary of the story you can manage. It has the skeleton of, but seldom is, a complete sentence. It must have a noun and a verb (the verb understood if not expressed). You omit articles, most adjectives and auxiliary verbs. You find the shortest words to do the job but try to avoid cliches. Observe how much economy this permits:

Complete sentence:

Merrill Scott has been appointed a member of the Central State University Board of Trustees by Governor Cripps.

Head:

Cripps names Scott to CSU Board

Avoid "label" heads, which have no verb. They fail to tell what the real news is. For example, you should not write:

Riot in Prospect Park today

but:

Police halt Prospect Park riot

Your responsibility as a headline writer includes, besides making sure the head fits and accurately summarizes the news, using vivid and forceful words so the reader will want to read the whole story.

Headlines are almost always written under pressure. You will have to make compromises and bend the rules sometimes. But try to keep these pointers in mind. Examples of poor heads are on the first line, better versions on the second.

1. Use strong verbs, active rather than passive. Use specific, not general nouns.

    Women found safe after accident

    Two women survive fall from tower

2. Don't leave out the subject.

    Resigns, then changes mind and returns

    Dean resigns, then changes mind

3. Each line should be a grammatical unit. Try not to end a line with a preposition. Avoid splitting verb parts. Don't split the modifier from the noun.

    Building plans told by
    County Commissioners

    Commissioners describe
    new public safety center

*Yanks and Mets will
contend in Series*

**Yanks and Mets
set for Series starter**

*Bay Area has sharp quake
but no damage*

**Quake hits Bay Area;
no damage reported**

4. Attribution: Just as in the body of the story, you must attribute every-
    thing not vouched for by the reporter as fact.

New tuition fees too high

Tuition too high, say students

Quotes are one way to do this if you don't have room in the head to tell who
said it. The quotes alert the reader to look in the story for the source. Always use
single quotes, to save space.

City will limit water use to meet 'disastrous' drought

Another way to show attribution is with a dash or colon, if the source is newsworthy and you don't have room for "says."

Drought 'worst ever'—mayor

Inflation to slow: Baker

5. Never use a period at the end of a head. Use semicolons inside the head
    to divide thoughts.

*City to vacate street.
Pedestrian mall planned.*

**City to vacate street;
pedestrian mall planned**

6. If you use abbreviations, be sure they are familiar.

API chairman predicts no serious oil shortages

Oil industry spokesman sees supplies adequate

7. Use the present tense ("historical present") or future; seldom past.

    Southeast Asia leaders met to discuss trade treaties

    Southeast Asia leaders meet to discuss trade treaties

11

Objectivity, fairness and accuracy

Traditionally, or at least for nearly a century, American journalism has prided itself on adherence to high standards in these areas.

Lately there has been a trend toward frankly opinionated reporting, or what is known as "advocacy journalism." This is fine, if the reader realizes ahead of time that an editorial point of view may be expressed or implied in what purport to be news stories.

However, in most of the country's newsrooms objectivity is still the ideal. So is the related quality of fairness (telling both sides).

You will do well to work toward being objective and fair in your newswriting, until it becomes second nature.

/ *BE OBJECTIVE*

Keep your personal opinion out of your story. You can't help having a point of view on most matters you write about. But don't let it show in your story.

First, don't use "I" or "me" in your writing. (Though you may do so in reviews, try not to overdo it. The reader already knows, since it is a signed review, that you're giving your personal opinion. No need to interject "I think" or "in my view," etc.)

Similarly, avoid "you" in newswriting, since it assumes a dialogue between reporter and reader. (This doesn't apply to feature stories.)

In advance news stories about campus events and activities it is sometimes hard to be objective if you yourself wish to promote the event—or if the person you interview about it urges you to promote it. The temptation may be strong to end your story on the next baseball game with something like:

The team really needs our support so everybody come out next Friday and show them we're behind them.

Or if a club officer asks you to include a plug for new members:

This is the first meeting of the year for the UFO Club; if you're curious, now would be a good time to see what it's all about. The club needs new members.

Neither of these actually used the first person, but it is implied by the use of "you." Would you see such writing in a metropolitan daily? Certainly not. So try to avoid it in the campus paper. A good way to get around it is to quote someone (the coach, the club officer), with a statement about the event, such as:

"There's room for 150 spectators in the bleachers," said Coach Samuels. "Since this is the last game of the season, I sure hope they'll be filled up."

// BE FAIR

Especially in reporting controversial, emotion-charged events such as strikes, protests and some speeches and meetings dealing with inflammatory matters, it is hard to avoid letting your own feelings creep in. Even if you are careful not to slant your reporting one way or another, you may, without really meaning to, give a lot of space to the side you favor or are more familiar with—and only scantily cover the other.

You must think of the story from the point of view of a reader who wants to know all the facts. Then talk to and listen to both sides and include everything that an objective observer would consider pertinent.

If you quote a spokesman for one side of an issue, do your best to get a statement from the other side. If you try and fail, tell your readers that, so they will be aware there is another side:

"The teachers' strike is a flagrant violation of a previously agreed-on contract, negotiated in good faith on our side," said School Board member Jocelyn Hills.

However, the spokesman for the teachers' union disagreed. Jerry Howard said the talks were broken off Friday by the School Board and that the union had no recourse but to call a strike.

(Or: Jerry Howard, president of the teachers' union, could not be reached for comment.)

The news columns of a paper are supposed to report the truth—the whole truth. The only place where anyone connected with the paper may properly express an opinion about the right or wrong of a situation is the editorial page.

/// *FINALLY: BE ACCURATE*

Rules about objectivity and fairness in newswriting may be broken or bent by good writers, but no one will deny that accuracy is absolutely and always essential.

Don't guess—at facts, at quotations, at spellings of names, at figures, at titles.

If you have the slightest doubt, whether because your notes aren't clear or you forgot to ask or your informant wasn't sure, or for any reason—check! This may require only one phone call, or a quick look at your newspaper's morgue, or it may take extensive research. But your first duty to your reader is to be accurate, about the little things as well as the big.

Don't report rumors as facts. Chase down the source. If you can't substantiate it leave it out. If you can, but it's not generally known or might be disputed, be sure to attribute it: tell who your source was and include a quote.

12

Basic journalism textbooks and reference works

TEXTBOOKS ON WRITING AND REPORTING

A Journalist's Guide to the Internet, by Christopher Callahan. Allyn & Bacon, 1999.

Reporting for the Media, by Fred Fedler and others. 7th edition. Oxford University Press, 2004.

The Elements of Newswriting, by James W. Kershner. Allyn & Bacon, 2005.

News Reporting and Writing, by Melvin Mencher. 8th edition. McGraw-Hill, 2000

Creative Interviewing: The Writer's Guide to Gathering Information by Asking Questions, by Ken Metzker. Allyn & Bacon, 1996.

USEFUL REFERENCE WORKS FOR THE JOURNALIST

(Most of these are revised and republished frequently.)

The Associated Press Stylebook and Briefing on Media Law. The Associated Press. New York.

A good dictionary, e.g., *Webster's New World Dictionary of the English Language.* William Collins—World Publishing Company. New York.

or

The American Heritage Dictionary of the English Language. American Heritage. New York.

Familiar Quotations, by John Bartlett. Little, Brown. New York.

The Elements of Style, by William Strunk, Jr. and E.B. White. Macmillan. New York. Penguin published an illustrated edition in 2005.

Chicago Manual of Style. University of Chicago Press. Chicago.

Roget's Thesaurus of English Words and Phrases. Crowell. New York. (Also available in paperback and dictionary form.)

Headlines and Deadlines: A Manual for Copy Editors, by Robert Garst and Theodore Bernstein. Columbia University Press. New York.

The World Almanac and Book of Facts. World Almanac Books. New York.

or

Information Please Almanac. Simon & Schuster. New York.

13

Newspaper terms

advance	A preliminary story on an event that has not yet happened.
agate type	Type that is 5–1/2 points in depth. *(See* point.)
A.P.	Associated Press, the press service.
art	All newspaper illustrations.
attribution	Telling the source of a story or fact, thus giving it authenticity.
bank	Part of headline; also called deck.
banner	A headline that runs the width of the page; also called streamer.
beat	A reporter's regular run, as the police beat, court house beat.
bf	Boldface (black) type.
body	Main part of the news story.
body type	Small type used for most of the paper.
box	An enclosure of line rules or borders.
break	(1) Noun: Point at which a story stops and is continued to another column or page. (2) Verb: To become available for publication.
bridge	The writer's device to take the reader from the lead into the body of the story.
byline	The writer's name, under the headline and before the story.
caps	Capital letters.
caption	Headline for picture or illustration (sometimes loosely used for cutline).
copy	All written material to be printed in the paper.
copy editor	One who edits stories and writes headlines.
credit line	Line acknowledging source of a story or picture.
cut	(1) Noun: Printed picture or illustration. (2) Verb: To reduce a story's length.
cutline	Explanatory text, usually under a picture.

dateline	Line at the beginning of a story, with the place and sometimes the date of origin.
deadline	Time when copy is due.
deck	Part of a multibank headline.
down style	Headline style which uses few capital letters.
ears	Small boxes to left and right of nameplate (flag).
edit	To revise, correct and improve a story.
editorialize	To include the writer's opinion in copy.
em	Unit to measure column width. The pica em is about 1/6 inch.
feature	A story that may, but need not, have a news peg, and usually depends on human or entertaining aspects for interest.
filler	Short news or informational item used to fill a small space in a page.
flag	Name of paper appearing on front page; also called nameplate, logo. (Not the same as masthead.)
follow, **follow-up**	Story with later news of an event already reported.
graf	Paragraph
handout	*See* release.
head	Short for headline.
insert	Copy to be inserted in a story already written.
jump	To continue a story from one page to another.
jump head	Headline for a continued story.
kicker	A short one-line head above the main head, usually slightly to the left; sometimes underlined or in italics, and usually in type about one-half the size of the main head.
1c	Lower case letters.
lead (lēd)	The first paragraph of a news story.
lead (lĕd)	(1) Noun: Originally, metal pieces placed between lines of type to add space; now, space between lines. (2) Verb: To add space between lines.
lower case	Not capital letters.

makeup	Arrangement of pictures, stories, ads, etc. on a page.
masthead	Editorial page heading, listing paper's name, address, officers, other information.
(more)	Used at end of a page of copy to indicate story is continued on the next page.
morgue	File for newspaper clippings, pictures, reference books, etc., that can give background for future stories; also called library.
nameplate	Name of paper on page one; also called flag, logo.
news peg	The significant point that makes a story newsworthy or interesting.
obit	Obituary; includes biographical details of the person.
pica	Unit of horizontal measurement, 1/6 inch.
point	Unit of vertical measurement, 1/72 inch, used to measure type. Most newspapers use 8–or 9–pt. body type.
release	(1) Instructions on when to publish a story, as "Release after 3 p.m. Feb. 2." (2) A non-staff-written story, sent to the newspaper by a press agent or public relations firm for a person, organization or group; also called handout.
rewrite man	One who writes a story from facts given by another reporter.
roundup	A story that puts together several aspects of a newsworthy event, or several stories of a related nature (as traffic accidents, weather).
rule	Line to separate columns and make borders and boxes.
running story	Story sent to compositors in sections.
scoop	An exclusive story.
sidebar	A related story that runs alongside the main story, with background, color, secondary details, etc.
slant	To emphasize a certain phase of a news event.
slugline	A short topical line at the beginning of a reporter's story to make it easy to identify; repeated on succeeding pages.
standard lead, summary lead	A lead that answers the questions "who, what, where, when, why, how."
stet	Literally, "let it stand"; a copyreader's and proofreader's sign, meaning to restore the material that has been marked out.

style	Accepted usage for spelling, punctuation, capitalization, abbreviations, etc.
stylebook	A written guide to style usage.
subhead	Small, one-line headline used in body of story.
suspended interest	A story with the main news or point at the end.
take	A section of a running story.
thirty	Usually typed thus: -30- to indicate end of story. Some writers use these endmarks: ###
upper case	Capital letters; also UC, caps.

14

Copy-editing symbols

The United States Coast Guard   abbreviate

will investigate a "fender bender"

accident that occured between the   insert letter

ferry "Washtucna" and a sailboat   delete punctuation

off Point Grosvenor yesterday.   transpose words

The Washtuccna, which steams   delete letter

on the Marblemount Port Washing-   insert punctuation

ton run, was in the south bound   close up

shipping lane and collided with the

sailboat Great Yarmouth, registered

in Jamaica, a C.G. spokesman said.   spell out

The spokesman said damage was

minor, but twelve passengers on   use numeral

the ferry were treated for lacera-

tions and bruises.   run in; bring copy
                                            together
The Marine Inspection Unit of   lower case

the coast guard is expected to   capitalize

investigate the causes of the acci-   delete words; close up

dent Monday morning, the spokes-

man said. According to a ferry   paragraph
                                            (or: ¶Acccording)
passenger, two persons were

visible on the Great Yarmouth deck

but niether of the 2 was at the tiller.   transpose letters,
                                            spell out
The Coast Guard was in-

formed of the incident by a radio

message from the acting captain of the   insert word

Washtucna, Barney Gomez.

Index

978-0-595-37484-7
0-595-37484-0

Printed in the United States
201400BV00004B/59/A